UNEARTHING ANCIENT CIVILIZATIONS

ANCIENT MESOPOTAMIA REVEALED

BY DONNA REYNOLDS

New York

Published in 2023 by Cavendish Square Publishing, LLC
29 E. 21st Street, New York, NY 10010

Copyright © 2023 by Cavendish Square Publishing, LLC

First Edition

No part of this publication may be reproduced, stored in a retrieval system, or transmitted in any form or by any means—electronic, mechanical, photocopying, recording, or otherwise—without the prior permission of the copyright owner. Request for permission should be addressed to Permissions, Cavendish Square Publishing, 29 E. 21st Street, New York, NY 10010. Tel (877) 980-4450; fax (877) 980-4454.

Website: cavendishsq.com

This publication represents the opinions and views of the author based on his or her personal experience, knowledge, and research. The information in this book serves as a general guide only. The author and publisher have used their best efforts in preparing this book and disclaim liability rising directly or indirectly from the use and application of this book.

All websites were available and accurate when this book was sent to press.

Library of Congress Cataloging-in-Publication Data

Names: Reynolds, Donna, 1976- author.
Title: Ancient Mesopotamia revealed / Donna Reynolds.
Description: New York : Cavendish Square Publishing, [2023] | Series: Unearthing ancient civilizations | Includes index.
Identifiers: LCCN 2021048712 | ISBN 9781502665942 (set) | ISBN 9781502665959 (library binding) | ISBN 9781502665935 (paperback) | ISBN 9781502665966 (ebook)
Subjects: LCSH: Iraq–History–To 634–Juvenile literature.
Classification: LCC DS71 .R49 2023 | DDC 935–dc23/eng/20211022
LC record available at https://lccn.loc.gov/2021048712

Editor: Jennifer Lombardo
Copyeditor: Abby Young
Designer: Deanna Paternostro

The photographs in this book are used by permission and through the courtesy of: Cover, back cover Iurii Kazakov/Shutterstock.com; p. 4 Peter Hermes Furian/Shutterstock.com; p. 7 Simon Edge/Shutterstock.com; pp. 8–9 Will Rodrigues/Shutterstock.com; p. 10 Interfoto/Alamy Stock Photo; p. 12, 28 (bottom) Dima Moroz/Shutterstock.com; pp. 14–15 De Luan/Alamy Stock Photo; p. 16 Viacheslav Lopatin/Shutterstock.com; p. 19 Isaac Mok/Shutterstock.com; p. 20 garanga/Shutterstock.com; p. 22 PhotoLohi/Shutterstock.com; pp. 24–25 Anna Azimi/Shutterstock.com; p. 26 Spiroview Inc/Shutterstock.com; p. 28 (top left) MehmetO/Shutterstock.com; p. 28 (top right) Essam al-Sudani/Shutterstock.com.

Some of the images in this book illustrate individuals who are models. The depictions do not imply actual situations or events.

CPSIA compliance information: Batch #CSCSQ23: For further information, contact Cavendish Square Publishing LLC, New York, New York, at 1-877-980-4450.

Printed in the United States of America

CONTENTS

CHAPTER ONE	5
THE CRADLE OF CIVILIZATION	
CHAPTER TWO	11
THE RISE OF EMPIRES	
CHAPTER THREE	17
TWO BABYLONS	
CHAPTER FOUR	23
THE END OF MESOPOTAMIA	
HISTORY HAPPENED HERE	28
EVENTS DURING ANCIENT MESOPOTAMIA	29
GLOSSARY	30
FIND OUT MORE	31
INDEX	32

The shaded part of this map shows roughly where ancient Mesopotamia was. It wasn't one country but a group of civilizations.

CHAPTER ONE
THE CRADLE OF CIVILIZATION

Ancient Mesopotamia is the name of an area where the world's oldest recorded civilizations were formed, which is why it is sometimes called the cradle of civilization. It was located between the Tigris and Euphrates Rivers in southwestern Asia. This is why it was named Mesopotamia, which means "between rivers" in Greek. Ancient Mesopotamia included parts of the modern countries of Turkey, Syria, Iraq, Iran, and Kuwait.

THE ANCIENT SUMERIANS

Around 5000 BCE, a group of people called the Sumerians began farming in southeast Mesopotamia. They built **irrigation** systems to bring water to their crops. The land was so good for farming that many people moved there. As the population grew, the towns turned into cities. With so many people living in one place, the Sumerians needed to create a system of government to help keep order.

Sumer was not one single country. Instead, it was a group of city-states. A city-state was a city that controlled nearby farms and villages. Each city-state was independent, which

5

meant it ruled itself. An example of a modern-day city-state is Singapore.

OLDER THAN HISTORY

People settled in the Mesopotamia area around 14,000 BCE. However, these settlements were not considered civilizations yet because people lived in small villages at first. It was not until about 5000 BCE that the villages grew big enough to be called towns and cities. This is why people say the history of ancient Mesopotamia starts around that time.

THE SUMERIAN WAY OF LIFE

The Sumerians created the first documented major city in the world. It was called Uruk, and it was settled in about 4500 BCE. Experts think there might be older cities, but only Uruk kept records we can read. From these records, we know what life was like there, when it was settled, and what was made and traded there. Other Sumerian city-states that were formed after Uruk included Ur, Nippur, and Kish. These were all smaller than Uruk. Experts think Uruk might have been the biggest city in the world by 2800 BCE.

Sumerian city-states were independent, but many things were shared among them. Each city-state had a **ziggurat** in the center, which was both a temple and a place for people to gather. Religion—having a belief system—was very important to the Sumerians, and each city-state had its own special gods and goddesses, as well as the main ones that all Sumerians believed in. The city-states also shared a common language and **culture**.

6

This ziggurat marks what was once the center of the city of Ur in present-day Iraq.

IMPORTANT INVENTIONS

The Sumerians invented many things that changed life forever and that are still used today. One of these was the wheel! Wheels were first used to make pottery. It was not until about 300 years after they were invented that they were used for **transportation**. The Sumerians also invented the sailboat, which helped them move goods and people along the Tigris and Euphrates Rivers.

This is an example of cuneiform writing.

The Sumerians also created the first calendar system and the first way of telling time. Even today, we use their system: A day is 24 hours, with about 12 hours of day and 12 hours of night; a minute has 60 seconds; and an hour has 60 minutes. The number 60 was used because that was the base of the system of mathematics the Sumerians invented. They used this system to record information about their crops and the goods they traded.

Sumerian cities became important centers for trade. The people traded cloth, tools, and the extra grain they grew. To keep track of their traded goods, the Sumerians created the first known writing system in the world. It was called cuneiform, and it used more than 600 wedge-shaped **symbols**. These symbols were pressed into soft clay tablets.

9

This metal statue of the head of Akkadian ruler Sargon the Great is in the Iraq Museum in Baghdad.

CHAPTER TWO
THE RISE OF EMPIRES

Even though they were similar in many ways, the Sumerian city-states fought against each other almost constantly. Because they did not work together very much, it was easy for outsiders to **invade** and take over. This was a big part of why the Sumerian civilization did not last.

THE FALL OF SUMER

While the Sumerians were living in the southern part of Mesopotamia, the Akkadians were living in a city-state called Akkad in the north. Between 2400 and 2300 BCE, the Akkadian ruler, King Sargon (also known as Sargon the Great), **conquered** the Sumerians and created what's believed to be the first-ever empire. The two cultures combined into one, and most people in the empire learned how to speak both Sumerian and Akkadian.

After the Akkadians took over Sumer, they continued to make their empire bigger. They fought and conquered other groups around Mesopotamia. By about 2240 BCE, the empire stretched for about 800 miles (1,290 kilometers) and included the areas that are now Anatolia, Iran, Arabia, and the Mediterranean.

This carved rock shows King Naram-Sin leading the Akkadian army to victory in a battle to add land to the Akkadian Empire.

LIFE IN THE AKKADIAN EMPIRE

The Akkadian Empire was huge and was made up of several different cultures, so life was not exactly the same everywhere. However, some things were shared across the empire. The rulers improved irrigation systems, built roads to connect cities, and created the first system for sending mail.

Social classes were also the same throughout the empire. The highest class included merchants, teachers, and shipbuilders. Under them were bakers, farmers, artists, soldiers, sailors, and many others. The lowest class was enslaved people. Slavery in Mesopotamia was not based on race. A person could become enslaved by being captured in war, being kidnapped and sold, or as punishment for a crime.

POWERFUL WOMEN

Priestesses were some of the most powerful and respected people in Mesopotamia. They could read, which was a skill most women were not taught. King Sargon's daughter, the priestess Enheduanna, is the world's first author whose name we know. Many priestesses were also taught how to heal. The world's first doctors and dentists were Sumerian and Akkadian priestesses.

THE BABYLONIANS

After about 200 years, the Akkadian Empire fell. Historians now think a big reason for this was a **drought** in the northern part of Mesopotamia that started around 2200 BCE and lasted for 300 years. People in the north moved down to the south, which made the cities very crowded. They started fighting each other, which made the empire weak. Around 2150 BCE, it **collapsed**.

The Sumerian city of Ur took power again for a short time. Then, around 1900 BCE, a group called the Amorites conquered the city of Babylon.

Babylon remained a small kingdom until the sixth king, a man named Hammurabi, took power in about 1792 BCE. Under his rule, the kingdom took over all of southern Mesopotamia, and it became the Babylonian Empire.

A FORGOTTEN CIVILIZATION

After the Amorites came to power, the civilization of Sumer was

This drawing shows what Babylon may have looked like after Hammurabi took power.

no more. It had already partly disappeared during the Akkadian Empire. The Babylonian Empire had its own culture, and that spread through southern Mesopotamia when Hammurabi took over the area. The Sumerians were then forgotten. No one even knew they had existed until the 1840s. People went to the area of Mesopotamia at that time to try to find items from Babylon, and while they were there, they found items from Sumer as well.

This carving shows Assyrian king Ashurbanipal. Under his rule, the Assyrian Empire became the largest in the world at the time.

CHAPTER THREE
TWO BABYLONS

The Babylonian Empire did not last as long as other empires, but it made a lasting mark on history. After it was taken over by a group called the Assyrians, power changed hands again, and a new Babylonian Empire rose.

THE CODE OF HAMMURABI

To bring together the different groups of people in the Babylonian Empire, Hammurabi created laws for everyone to follow. The Code of Hammurabi was one of the first sets of written laws, but it was not written on paper. It was carved on a large stone called a stele. Some of its 282 laws were very **harsh**. For example, one of the most famous laws says that if one person hurts another, they should be hurt in the same way. This is where the saying "an eye for an eye" comes from. However, it was also the first set of laws to say that a person should not be punished until they are proven guilty.

THE RISE OF THE ASSYRIANS

The Assyrians, like the Sumerians, lived in a group of independent city-states. However, the Sumerians focused

17

mainly on advancing science and art, while the Assyrians focused on war. Because they had better weapons than other Mesopotamian groups, the Assyrians mostly kept control of their lands in the north, even when the Babylonian Empire was in control in the south. Over time, as other groups fought for control of the Babylonian Empire, Assyria continued to grow. Around 900 BCE, Assyria became the most powerful force in the region. With its advanced weapons and skilled army, it conquered the lands around it to become a large empire.

By 671 BCE, the Assyrians had conquered all of Mesopotamia and much of the Middle East, including parts of modern-day Egypt, Israel, and Jordan. However, this made their empire too big to control. A new group of Babylonians, as well as a group called the Medes, attacked Assyria. These attacks caused it to fall in 612 BCE.

A BIBLICAL CITY

The Christian religion was not created until the first century CE, but when the Bible was written, it mentioned some of the history of ancient Mesopotamia. This is how historians knew these places had existed even after they disappeared. Ancient Sumer is not in the Bible, which is why it was forgotten. One of the most important Biblical cities was Nineveh, which the Assyrians made the capital of their empire around 700 BCE.

THE NEW BABYLONIAN EMPIRE

Before the Assyrian Empire fell, a group called the Chaldeans conquered Babylon, making them the new Babylonians. After the

The Ishtar Gate—part of which is shown here—was built during the Second Babylonian Empire.

This drawing shows what the Hanging Gardens of Babylon may have looked like, based on what people wrote about them.

Chaldeans conquered Assyria, their ruler, Nebuchadnezzar II, rebuilt the city of Babylon and made it the capital of their new empire in 626 BCE. This empire is known today by several names: the Chaldean Empire, the New Babylonian Empire, and the Second Babylonian Empire. This was a time of great wealth and power in Babylon, and the beautiful city became a center for science.

One of the most famous parts of the New Babylonian Empire may never have existed! Ancient Greeks and Romans wrote about the Hanging Gardens of Babylon. Mesopotamia was said to be the first place where people made gardens just because they were pretty, not to grow food. The Hanging Gardens were supposedly some of the most beautiful and **exotic** in the world. Some historians think the gardens were just a myth. Others think they were actually found at Nineveh. So far, the stories are the only proof that the gardens might have existed. We may never know the truth.

Cyrus the Great of Persia is buried here in Pasargadae, Iran.

CHAPTER FOUR
THE END OF MESOPOTAMIA

After Nebuchadnezzar II died, the New Babylonian Empire started to fall apart. This made it easy for a group called the Persians, led by Cyrus the Great, to conquer it around 550 BCE. The Persian Empire was one of the largest in history. It is also sometimes called the Achaemenid Empire after Achaemenes, who ruled the land of Persis from 705 to 675 BCE. It stretched more than 3,000 miles (4,830 km) and included not only Mesopotamia but also modern-day Egypt and Israel.

AN IMPORTANT CULTURE

The capital of the Persian Empire was created around 518 BCE by a ruler called Darius I. It was called Persepolis, which means "Persian city" in Greek, and it was located in modern-day Iran. Today, it is considered one of the world's most important historical places because of its amazing art and buildings.

The Persians also started Zoroastrianism—one of the world's oldest monotheistic religions. Monotheism means believing in one god. Before Zoroastrianism, which historians think started sometime between 1500 and 500 BCE, Mesopotamians were polytheistic. This means they believed in more than one god.

23

This two-headed statue of a griffin still stands in the ruins of Persepolis.

The Persians were also known for their beautiful art. They made things to use, to wear, and to look at out of gold, silver, and other metals. Many of their metal items had a griffin on them. This is a mythical animal with the wings and head of an eagle and the body of a lion. The griffin was the symbol of Persepolis.

DIVIDING THE EMPIRE

Because the Persian Empire was so large, it was impossible for one central government to keep control. The Persians knew other empires had fallen that way. To fix this problem, the empire was split into 20 to 30 areas. Each area was controlled by a governor called a satrap.

THE FALL OF THE PERSIAN EMPIRE

In 480 BCE, Greece tried to conquer Persia. The Persians won, but the war was so

This sculpture of Alexander the Great can be seen in the British Museum in London.

A TOLERANT RULER

For most of history up to the Persian Empire, when a new group took control, the new leaders made everyone they conquered follow their culture and religion. Cyrus the Great was the first to let people do what they wanted as long as they followed the laws of the empire and paid their taxes. This made the Persian Empire a very peaceful place to live.

expensive that the empire never fully recovered. This made it easy for a ruler named Alexander the Great to conquer Persia in 330 BCE. By this time, much of the culture of ancient Mesopotamia had been lost because of the number of times it had been conquered. When Alexander conquered the Persian Empire, he mixed the Persian culture with Greek culture. This is often seen as the end of ancient Mesopotamian civilizations.

HISTORY HAPPENED HERE

PERSEPOLIS

- The ruins of the city can be found near a mountain called Kuh-e Rahmat in Iran.
- A beautiful palace was built at Persepolis, but the city was hard to get to, so the rulers did not live there all the time.
- Alexander the Great set most of the city on fire to destroy it after he conquered it.

URUK

- Uruk was one of the first major cities in the world.
- The ruins of the city can be found 168 miles (270 km) south of Baghdad in Iraq.
- It was rediscovered in 1849 CE. Workers spent the next few years uncovering the ancient ruins.

STELE OF HAMMURABI

- The stele is in the Louvre Museum in Paris.
- The top shows Hammurabi on the left being given the laws by the Babylonian sun god, Shamash.
- The laws are written below in cuneiform.

28

EVENTS DURING
ANCIENT MESOPOTAMIA

CA. 5000 BCE Sumerian villages start to grow into cities, thanks to irrigation.

CA. 4500 BCE The world's first big city, Uruk, is created.

CA. 2300s BCE The Akkadians conquer the Sumerians, and the Akkadian Empire rises.

CA. 2150 BCE The Akkadian Empire falls.

CA. 1900 BCE The Amorites choose Babylon as their capital, and the Babylonian Empire rises.

1792 BCE Hammurabi becomes the king of Babylon.

900 BCE The Assyrians rise to power.

671 BCE The Assyrians control all of Mesopotamia and much of the Middle East.

626 BCE The New Babylonian Empire rises.

550 BCE The Persian Empire conquers Babylon.

330 BCE Alexander the Great conquers the Persian Empire.

GLOSSARY

collapse: To break apart or fail.

conquer: To take by force.

culture: The beliefs and ways of life of a group of people.

drought: A long period of dry weather.

exotic: Different or unusual; relating to a plant or animal from a different part of the world.

harsh: Severe or cruel.

invade: To enter by force.

irrigation: The watering of a dry area by man-made means in order to grow plants.

symbol: A picture, shape, or object that stands for something else.

transportation: A way of traveling from one place to another.

ziggurat: An ancient Mesopotamian temple in the shape of a pyramid with steps on the outside.

FIND OUT MORE

BOOKS

Oakes, Lorna. *Step into Mesopotamia*. Leicester, UK: Southwater, 2020.

Randolph, Joanne. *Living and Working in Ancient Mesopotamia*. New York, NY: Enslow Publishing, 2018.

Tyler, Madeline. *Ancient Mesopotamia*. New York, NY: KidHaven Publishing, 2019.

WEBSITES

The British Museum: Mesopotamia
www.mesopotamia.co.uk/menu.html
This website has information about ancient Mesopotamia as well as activities to help visitors see what life was like back then.

Ducksters: Ancient Mesopotamia
www.ducksters.com/history/mesopotamia/ancient_mesopotamia.php
This website contains articles covering many topics about ancient Mesopotamia, including important inventions, famous people, and daily life.

***National Geographic*: Ancient Mesopotamia 101**
www.nationalgeographic.org/video/ancient-mesopotamia-101
This short video gives an overview of life in ancient Mesopotamia.

Publisher's note to educators and parents: Our editors have carefully reviewed these websites to ensure that they are suitable for students. Many websites change frequently, however, and we cannot guarantee that a site's future contents will continue to meet our high standards of quality and educational value. Be advised that students should be closely supervised whenever they access the internet.

INDEX

A

Achaemenid Empire, 23
Akkadian Empire/ Akkadians, 11, 13, 14–15
Alexander the Great, 26, 27
Amorites, 14
Assyrian Empire/ Assyrians, 17–18, 21

B

Babylonian Empire, 14, 15, 17, 18

C

Chaldean Empire/ Chaldeans, 18–21
city-states, 5–6, 11, 17
Code of Hammurabi, 17
cuneiform writing, 9
Cyrus the Great, 23, 27

D

Darius I, 23

E

Enheduanna, 13

H

Hammurabi, 14, 17
Hanging Gardens of Babylon, 21

I

inventions, 7–9

K

Kish, 6

M

Medes, 18

N

Nebuchadnezzar II, 21, 23
New Babylonian Empire, 21, 23
Nineveh, 18, 21
Nippur, 6

P

Persepolis, 23, 25
Persian Empire/ Persians, 23–27
priestesses, 13

R

religion, 6, 18, 23

S

Sargon the Great, 11, 13
Second Babylonian Empire, 21
slavery, 13
Sumer/Sumerians, 5, 6, 7, 9, 11, 13, 14, 15, 17–18

T

trade, 6, 9

U

Ur, 6, 14
Uruk, 6

Z

Zoroastrianism, 23